BEGINNER'S BASKETBALL

BEGINNER'S BASKETBALL

Bill Beswick

KAYE & WARD LTD
In Association with Peter Crawley

Text Copyright © 1983 by Bill Beswick

Published 1983 by
Kaye & Ward Ltd
The Windmill Press,
Kingswood, Tadworth, Surrey

ISBN 0 7182 1740 3

All enquiries and requests relevant
to this title should be sent
to the publishers at the above
address and not to the printer.

Printed in England by
Whitstable Litho Ltd.,
Whitstable, Kent

CONTENTS

Acknowledgements

The author wishes to thank these people concerned with getting him "started in basketball": his brother Fred for introducing him to the game at Manchester Y.M.C.A., and Kamel Tober, Wilf Byrne, and Bill Steel for helping him understand and love the game.

The author is also greatly indebted to the persistence and support of his wife Val, the typing of Joy Derbyshire, the photographic work of Peter Realf, Trevor Pountain, and Jeff Booton, and for the general assistance of all at Stockport Belgrade Basketball Club.

Useful Addresses

For beginners who require more information, the following sources may be useful:

The English Basketball Association,
Calomax House,
Lupton Avenue,
Leeds 9

National League Division One Clubs

Birmingham Bullets

Mr. R. J. Hope
St. Peter's College,
Saltley,
Birmingham
B8 3TE

Bracknell Pirates

Mrs. P. J. West
76 Woodbridge Road,
Guildford,
Surrey

Brighton Bears

The Secretary
130 Queens Road,
Brighton,
Sussex
BN1 3WB

Crystal Palace

Mrs. P. Last
Crystal Palace Basketball Club,
Crystal Palace National
Sports Centre,
Ledrington Road,
London SE19

John Carr Doncaster Panthers

Mr. M. A. Wordsworth
4 Exchange Buildings,
Market Place,
Doncaster
DN1 1NF

Ovaltine Rebels
Hemel Hempstead

Mr. R. C. Yapp
Dacorum Sports Centre,
Park Road,
Hemel Hempstead,
Herts

Club Cantabrica Kingston

Mr. P. Herlihy
Tolworth Recreation Centre,
Fullers Way North,
Surbiton,
Surrey

Planters Leicester

Mr. G. D. Blatherwick
LAS Basketball Ltd.,
2nd Floor
41 Granby Street,
Leicester

Wakewood Liverpool

Mr. C. J. Bentley
2nd Floor,
Union Building,
21 Victoria Street,
Liverpool
L1 6BS

Manchester Giants

Mrs. J. Atkinson
207 Bramhall Lane,
Davenport,
Stockport
SK2 6JA

Solent Stars

Mr. H. Smith
Solent Stars Limited,
33a London Road,
Southampton

Sunderland

Mr. D. Elderkin
21 Foyle Street,
Sunderland,
Tyne and Wear

Warrington Lada Vikings

Mrs. C. Honeybone
Birchwood Basketball Club,
56/58 Benson Road,
Birchwood,
Warrington
WA3 7PW

Introduction

Basketball is a game that has given me much pleasure,
but none more so than seeing that pleasure increasingly
shared as the game has spread in popularity to the point
today where it is an important part of secondary schools'
physical education curriculum, and local, regional, and
national leagues are all firmly established. In the last
decade we have seen the advent of mini-basketball for
junior school children, women's basketball, and the
heavily sponsored basketball of the National League.

There is much for the newcomer to the game to aspire
to and the indications are that more and more people —
boys and girls, players and coaches — are starting
basketball. This book aims to help the starters understand
the game, its techniques and tactics, and allow them to
participate fully from their first moment of involvement in
this great game.

Bill Beswick

Chapter One

What is Basketball?

One of the key factors in basketball's popularity is that it is a simple game in essence but very demanding to play. The objective of the game is quite simply to put the ball through your opponent's hoop more times than he manages to put it through yours. However, the development of certain key rules limits the way in which we are allowed to achieve this.

KEY RULES — NO CONTACT — in order that skills flourish players are not allowed to tackle opponents to win the ball.

Rule 9. 'A player shall not hold, push, charge, trip, impede the progress of an opponent by extending his arm, shoulder, hip, or knee, or by bending his body into other than normal position, nor use any rough tactics.'

Any player who does use 'rough tactics' does not usually stay in the game long because each player is only allowed five fouls before he must leave the court and take no further part in the game.

ONE PACE — but if the defence can't tackle then neither can the offence run with the ball. When a player takes possesion of the ball he is limited to one pace. He can take that pace, however, in any direction he wishes by 'pivoting' on his back foot. Successful pivoting keeps the ball protected from the defender who moves in to guard very closely.

ONE DRIBBLE — the offensive player is allowed to progress with the ball but he must dribble the ball in order to change his position on the floor. Once he has picked up the ball at the end of the dribble he can't dribble again until another player on court has touched the ball.

Basketball now begins to appear as a minimal contact game dependent on good footwork, good ball skills, and good movement both with and without the ball. In itself this does not yet demand a great deal from the starter. Any school playground in Britain can show wonderful examples of children running, changing direction and pace, stopping suddenly, and dribbling, throwing, catching, and aiming balls of varying sizes. Playing basketball only demands that we do these simple things well — the higher the standard the better we need to do them.

To perform simple skills well means a combination of ability, practice, and coaching. We are all limited by our ability level and the coaching available for us but all our starters should be able to practise sufficiently for their skills to improve. For the starter with ambition this is a must. However, one of the assets of basketball as a game is that it can be enjoyably practised alone. All one needs are a ring and a ball.

American and many European homes have basketball rings in the yard outside — often fixed on to the garage — as a natural plaything for children and this could be a very important factor in the development of good players in these countries.

Basketball does demand that we do simple things well but it also demands that we achieve them in co-operation with four other members of our team and in competition against the five members of the opposition. It is in the playing of the game that individual skill and effort is fully tested.

Understanding of the total game now becomes vital to our starter as he makes his way into the team. I have already said that basketball is a simple game in essence and the proof is that the starter only needs to understand the four key phases of the game to be ready to fit into a team pattern at a simple level.

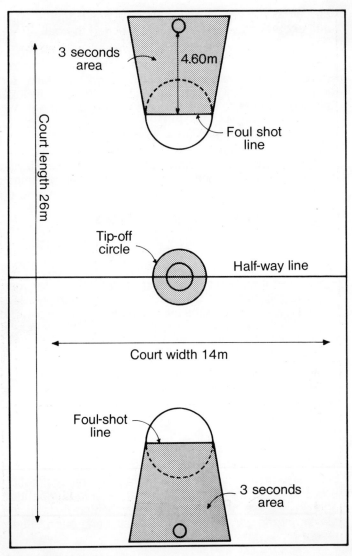

1   The basketball court markings

PRINCIPLES OF PLAY — POSSESSION — each team must work to win possession of the ball and then keep possession until a good shot is secured. Getting free and passing skills are vital here.

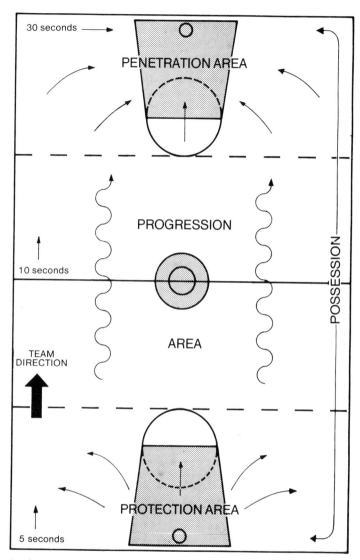

2   A tactical view of the basketball court

PROGRESSION — having gained possession the team has to progress the ball to the area around their opponents' basket where they can feel confident of scoring. Passing and dribbling skills ensure quick and controlled progression.

PENETRATION — obviously the nearer we are to our opponents' basket when we shoot the more chance we have of scoring, and so we must make some tactical moves which enable us to achieve this. Movement off the ball, passing, dribbling, are all important here — but especially the accurate shooting which makes penetration a success.

PROTECTION — as well as scoring we must work hard to prevent our opponents scoring, and we must learn to protect the vital area around our basket from penetration.

So the game is really quite simple — the team works hard to gain possession of the ball, progresses it down court, penetrates close enough to the opponents' basket for a good shot, and if possession is lost falls back quickly to protect their own basket. Understanding this and awareness of the various techniques involved in carrying out each phase successfully should set our starter well on the way.

But it is also important that the starter makes an effort to understand the structure of basketball in terms of playing regulations. This can be a most confusing part of starting basketball as there are many and varied regulations governing the game. These regulations, like the rules, have evolved to produce a better game. I would hope that a sympathetic teacher or coach would introduce them slowly and clearly, but briefly these are regulations I consider important to starters.

Playing Regulations

Officials — one referee and one umpire cover play between them.

Teams — ten players per team, five on court at any one time, up to five substitutes waiting on the team bench.

Time — two halves of twenty minutes each with the clock stopped when the officials stop play.

Scoring — two points for each basket scored during open play and one point for each foul shot scored.

The start — the game starts with a jump ball (tip-off) at the centre circle between two opponents.

After a score — the game does not stop but the defending team have five seconds to bring the ball back into play from the end line under their own basket.

Out of bounds — when a team causes the ball to go out of play, or commits a violation of the rules, possession is given to their opponents and they bring the ball back into play from the nearest point of the sideline.

Fouls — each player is allowed five fouls before he must cease to take part in the game.

Foul shots — when a player is fouled in the act of shooting he will receive foul (or penalty) shots. If the basket was scored anyway he receives only one bonus shot. If the shot had missed the player receives three attempts to score two points.

By now, the key rules and regulations of the game — as well as a working knowledge of the principles of play — should, hopefully, be firmly established. Obviously there are more rules and regulations important to our developing knowledge of the game but I intend to introduce those in the text where they are pertinent to the learning of techniques and tactics. This should also help explain how the rules evolved and hence improve understanding.

The beginner is now well prepared to go out on to the court and begin to enjoy the game of basketball. Chapter 2 will introduce him to the game in a group on the court.

Though this chapter may have more direct relevance to the teacher, the individual starter can still learn the need for and the application of differing techniques in the various phases of the game.

Chapter Two

Starting to Play

Our major objective when introducing the game of basketball must be to give the beginner as much information as he needs to get involved in the game — but not so much that he will be confused — and to structure the introductory phases so that all our starters will gain some success and satisfaction. To plunge them into the full game might well be disastrous. If basketball is a game of doing simple things well then we must adopt an approach which encourages this. In organising a simple introductory pattern of coaching, I follow three teaching principles:

1.   I always coach from the 'known to the unknown' so that our starters have always a basis for learning, a progression that avoids confusion.

2.   I attempt not to go beyond the ability level of the group (that generally means the weakest performers) and willingly restructure the game in any way necessary so that all starters can gain some form of initial success, encouraging them to go on and meet the increasing challenge of each phase of learning.

3.   People learn more when the learning is presented in an enjoyable manner.

The previous chapter shows clearly that the beginner to basketball must learn to gain and keep possession of the ball, progress it to a point on the court where penetration and scoring is possible, and then protect his basket from his opponents' attempt to score. My introduction for starters will reflect and reinforce those aspects through a variety of very enjoyable minor games.

(i) Possession Ball

Much of this work is based on the early pioneering work of Brian Coleman, Technical Director of the E.B.B.A., who first developed an educational approach to introducing the game, and I would wish to acknowledge that.

A simple way to get the group working in a basketball environment — and one well known to all starters already — is to play possession ball with a basketball. One team has to keep possession for as long as possible (the coach can set targets such as ten passes and count aloud) whilst their opponents seek to regain possession. The team in possession may not dribble the ball. The task of rules is to bring order from chaos and it will soon become clearly obvious that the two major rules of basketball need introducing *i.e. no contact and no running* with the ball. Possession ball will suddenly take on a more basketball-like structure and it is vital that the coach insists on these rules to create the correct habits in starters from the very beginning. Always remember in basketball that skill must win over force.

Coaching points:
- — use of space
- — signalling for the ball
- — good catching and passing
- — moving to get free
- — vision, seeing all the court
- — pivoting
- — 'loose' man for man marking

As the group improves and possession is held for longer and longer, split into smaller groups so that from a class of thirty playing fifteen a side we now have three games of five versus five in a more restricted space.

(ii) Wall Ball

Our two teams— or more if and when the coach feels it necessary — are now capable of basic possession skills and now we need to coach them to use that possession to make the progression up the court to a scoring position.

The player passing the ball has shown 'good vision' in seeing the
pass available, made good use of the pivot step to create the passing
opportunity around the very tall defender, and has chosen a good
pass, the bounce pass, to beat the defensive pressure. Notice the
defence, very close, yet causing no foul

Wall ball is a possession ball game (again no dribbling allowed) with a target — that of scoring by placing, not throwing, the ball anywhere on the wall that you are attacking. As it is only a slight adjustment it will not confuse the starters, and the simplicity of the scoring method allows even those of the weakest ability to gain the satisfaction of scoring.

Coaching points: — repeat possession ball skills
  — look ⎫
     move ⎬ down court to the target (wall)
     pass ⎭
  — defend in between opponents and target

By starting the game with a jump ball, and teaching how to restart from out of bounds and after a basket, we have moved considerably closer to the structure of the game proper.

(iii) Bench Ball

In order to move slightly closer to actual game demands of progression, penetration, and protection we can change the goal, in bench ball, from a wall to a target man. He stands on a bench or chair and is not allowed to move. So we have a possession ball game with the objective of progressing with the ball near enough to the target man to aim the ball high over the defence into his hands (whoever scores replaces the target man).

The natural inclination of players will be to crowd around the target man to get the easiest shot possible and a very tall starter will dominate and spoil the game. This then is a realistic and necessary time to introduce the players to the THREE-SECONDS RULE. A 'key-way' can be drawn in chalk around the target man in which the attacking players can only stay for three seconds when their team is in possession. If the coaches call this rule strictly the area around the basket will clear and be open for penetration moves.

The game begins with a jump ball, known as the 'tip off'

Coaching points:
— repeat possession ball skills
— repeat progression ball skills
— early basics of shooting
— possible zone defence
protecting target man

(iv) Points Ball

This game takes the starters two more steps forward, and virtually to the full game, by introducing dribbling, and shooting at the basket. Initially the game is similar to bench ball but the target is now the basket — which scores ten points, the ring — five, or the backboard — one point. Once a score is made the ball is dead and brought in from the end line. The winning team is the first to score twenty-one points. Notice that although the starters are now aiming for the basket there is a wide enough scoring scope for all ability levels to gain some success — the backboard is 183 by 122 centimetres (six feet by four feet).

By now teams should be reduced in numbers to five and be playing in a reasonably sized space, if not a full basketball court, and a number of situations will arise where a dribble forward would be the correct move for the player to make. At this stage I would introduce dribbling, noting the double dribble rule, and explaining very carefully the rather limited use of the dribble — to move forward when a pass forward is not available. Coaches must be very careful at this stage that licence to dribble does not spoil the possession skills gained in previous practices, and they must only make this move forward when assured that their starters have a firm foundation of possession skills.

Coaching points: —   repetition of previous learning
                        —   more shooting guidance
                        —   more defence guidance
                        —   dribbling skill — action
                                           — vision
                                           — ambidexterity

(v) Continuous Basketball

Time for the real game! But of course the 'real game' is only the combination of the phases that our starters have already been introduced to. Coaches will note that I continually stress repetition of previous learning. This is essential so that skills can develop into habits and thus when the beginner finally makes his appearance on court in a game he has a whole series of game habits to fall back on. A second point to note is the timing of moving our starters on from one phase of development to the next. There must be sufficient time given to each phase for the starter to undergo the necessary learning but the coach must not dwell too long for fear of losing motivation.

When our starters finally play the full game the coach must use every opportunity to reinforce previous learning and must be an observer/participant rather than a spectator. Continuous basketball is a means of playing the full game with a large number of players and keeping them all involved as much as possible. Two teams of five or three (the lower the number the greater the player involvement) play to score one basket. The winning team stays on but changes direction, bringing the ball in immediately from the end line where they have just scored. Meanwhile the losing team goes off court to the end of the waiting line of players while the team from the front of the line rushes on and takes up defensive positions. If nobody scores within one minute, change both teams and start with a tip-off.

Thus the game is introduced to starters in a clear, simple, progressive, and enjoyable manner. Although differing levels of ability will begin to be apparent between the starters, I would hope that all ability levels could find this approach a satisfying one. As the group reach the stage of playing the full game it will become clearly obvious that what is needed now is to abstract those skills from the game that are weak, practise them in isolation, and then reintroduce them to the game, thus constantly improving the game performance. The following chapters examine in more detail how this may be achieved.

Chapter Three

Improving Playing Skills

All starters will have developed a general level of skill at throwing and catching, aiming, dribbling the ball, and running and jumping. Playing basketball places great demand on these skills and as the standard of play improves so must the beginner's level of skill. Ability, good coaching, and practice are the keys and the starter must be willing to commit himself to the hard work of practice in order to improve — though basketball is fortunate in that practice can be good fun as well as hard work. Our understanding of the game indicates clearly those skills on which the starter must concentrate and we will now examine them in detail.

Possession Skills

Teams regain possession of the ball mostly after their opponents attempt a shot at basket, either scoring or missing. In order to make their own attempt at scoring that team has to use its new possession of the ball to progress the twenty metres or so down the court to a good shooting position.

RULES

This sequence of progression has to be completed within certain time limits imposed by three important rules of the game.

The five seconds rule allows the player with the ball, when guarded closely, only five seconds possession before he must take action. The ten seconds rule allows a team only ten seconds to progress the ball over the half-way line, and once over it may not come back during that offence. The whole sequence of progression and eventual shot at basket is limited by the thirty seconds rule to that amount of time and you will see thirty seconds timing devices placed near the court where players can constantly see them.

Five Seconds Rule: 'Held ball shall be called when a closely guarded player who is holding the ball does not pass, shoot . . . or dribble within 5 seconds.'

Ten Seconds Rule: 'When a team gains control of the ball in its back court it must within ten seconds cause the ball to go into its front court.'

Thirty Seconds Rule: 'When a team gains control of the ball on the court a try for goal must be made within thirty seconds.'

PASSING: THE KEY TO TEAM SUCCESS

Such rules are what makes basketball the fast and exciting game to play and watch that it is, but they also place great demands on our skills — and in this case the key skill of *passing*. The sequence described of gaining possession, progressing down court, penetrating the defence, and eventually scoring could be achieved by one player dribbling all the way and taking the shot — but what a wonderful player he would be! Many starters feel that this is what they must do when they gain possession of the ball, but all that happens, of course, is that five defenders can now mark the one man with the ball and he is easily dispossessed.

Passing is essential to the successful completion of the sequence because:

— it is the *safest* form of maintaining possession until a shot can be taken.

— a pass is *quicker* down court than a dribble.

— a pass can reach *anywhere* on court and so the defenders must mark every man — and with the defence spread there are many more gaps to penetrate.

Whether a starter at basketball or the best player in the National Basketball League, your success on court will be dependent on your ability to pass the ball well. The ability to dribble or shoot are, of course, of vital importance to individual prowess, but the majority of times a player receives the ball in a game he is in a position to do neither. He must then pass the ball to a team-mate in a better position and assist him to score the basket. The top players, often the smaller, quicker guards, can draw two or three defenders to them deliberately in order that they might make the pass to the then unmarked team-mate in a scoring position.

GOOD PASSING
There are certain basic problems each pass must overcome:

There are five defenders trying to prevent/intercept the pass — including one very close to you. The distance to be passed may vary from one metre to up to twenty-six metres. Either or both the passer and receiver may be on the move.

To overcome these a good pass must be:

Accurate

Well-timed — especially if the receiver is moving quickly

Direct — quickness prevents stealing — NO LOBS!

Flexible — able to pass in any direction at any speed

Adaptable — the right pass for the right occasion.

There are many types of basketball passes available to the starter but he should concentrate on the three most basic, consistent, and essential passes — the CHEST pass, the BOUNCE pass, and the OVERHEAD pass.

TECHNIQUE
These three passes are fairly easy for the starter to learn and all three are based on similiar principles.

— All start from the same basic position of readiness.

— All use two hands.

— All are whole body co-ordination passes but with special emphasis on full arm extension and wrist snap — the bending back of the hand at the wrist then snapping it sharply forward.

It is important that the basketball player in possession of the ball is always prepared to be able to pass quickly — therefore he should establish a position of readiness, while he decides his course of action. The position of readiness for a basketball player has five essentials:

1.   Ball held in two hands, thumbs behind ball (almost touching), fingers spread along sides.

2.   Elbows bent — tucked into sides, not outwards.

3.   Body balanced, relaxed, knees slightly bent, one foot slightly in front of the other.

4.   Always face the basket you are attacking.

5.   Give yourself the widest range of vision possible — and therefore the widest choice of passes — by using your pivot step to turn you around so you may see *all* your team-mates.

From the position of readiness a *chest* pass is easily executed using the following technique:

1.   Eyes on target.

2.   Aim for receiver's outside hand — hand furthest from defender.

3.   Extend arms, wrists and fingers toward receiver.

4.   Follow through with arms, snap on wrists.

5.   If distance or strength is needed step forward, use whole body to snap ball to receiver.

Position of readiness

Chest pass

Bounce pass

Overhead pass

The *bounce* pass is essentially the same as the chest pass, the only difference being that the body leans and the arms extend downwards creating a skidding pass that bounces about two-thirds of the way to the receiver and up into his hands.

For the *overhead* pass, from the position of readiness the ball is taken up over the head (note — not behind the head as in a soccer throw) and held as high as possible. The body stretches and the wrist and fingers snap and follow through to send the ball directly to the receiver's free hand.

Performed well, the chest, bounce and overhead passes meet most of the situations the starter at basketball will find himself in. The only other pass he needs to develop is for the situation where a team-mate is free but a long way off — too far for the other passes.

The *baseball* or *javelin* pass is an efficient method of passing the ball a long distance. To perform this:

1.   Turn sideways.

2.   Take ball back in one hand and with a flexed arm behind your shoulder.

3.   Release with full arm extension, snap of wrist, and body weight forward onto front foot. Just imagine pitching a baseball or throwing a javelin and you will accomplish this pass fairly quickly.

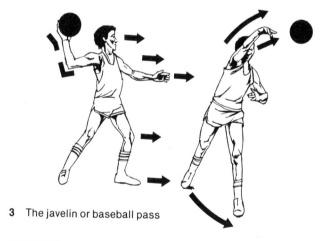

3   The javelin or baseball pass

PASSING IN THE GAME

With a little practice these passes can be executed well enough to help the beginner fit into the game situation. But as every National League or local club player can tell you — making a pass in practice and making one in the game is not quite the same. In the game your own defender is close up trying to force a mistake and all the team-mates that you are trying to pass to will have defenders just waiting to intercept a poor pass. The successful pass in the game depends on:

— The receiver working to get free and away from the defender to make the target easier.

— The passer choosing the right pass for the situation

These are the keys to passing skill when starting basketball but such skill will not be accomplished without good and regular practice. Listed below are a variety of practices that help develop passing skill whether working against the garage wall on your own or in a sports hall with a group of other starters.

1. Passing against a wall

— increase distance away from the wall.

— vary type of pass; increase speed of pass (how many in thirty seconds?).

— improve accuracy; pass into circle sixty centimetres (two feet) in diameter, drawn one and a half metres (five feet) up a wall, from a distance of two and a half metres (eight feet).

— pass at angle so you can receive ball back while on the move; also catching practice.

2. Passing in pairs

— stationary; vary pass, distance, aim for signalling hand. moving; pass in front of receiver.

3. Passing in three's

— stationary; vary direction / type /

The passer reacts to the position of the defender by choosing an overhead pass

The passer pivots away from the defensive pressure and gets the ball past the arms of the defenders by choosing a bounce pass

distance.
moving up and down gym.

— pass and follow.

— 'pig in the middle' (two attackers, one defender trying to steal ball).

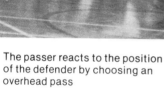

4. Passing in four's

— two against two possession ball; two with ball keep possession as long as possible while other two attempt to steal ball.

— shuttle passing;
the two's stand
opposite, three and a
half metres (twelve
feet) apart, and the ball
is passed across (vary
type of pass) and
passer always follows
line of pass to join
back of far line.

5. Passing in five's or more

one ball square drill;
— one person at each
corner of the square
and the ball is passed
around the square
while on the move
towards the next
corner. Increase the
size of the square until
you can pass the ball
round the 'square' half
of a basketball court.

With good passing skill our starter should be able to play his part in helping his team keep possession. Possession, however, may only last up to thirty seconds in basketball before a shot must be taken. Although the percentage of shots missed decreases as the standard of the game increases, it is still true to say that at most levels of play one shot out of every two will rebound out from the ring or backboard.

REGAINING POSSESSION of these missed shots is vital to both teams. The defence must prevent the offence securing the ball in a very good position under their basket, and they must win the ball in order to launch an attack. The offensive team know that if they secure second or third attempts on each shot at basket they are in a very strong position to dominate the game.

REBOUNDING

The starter must play his part in the rebounding efforts of his team, gaining and regaining possession whenever possible.
Rebounding skill is based on four factors:

1. Size.
2. Jumping ability.
3. Determination.
4. Technique.

Learners cannot do much about their size — tall players will always have the advantage — but they can work on the other three factors. Jumping ability can be improved by vigorous and constant jumping practice and a certain amount and type of weight training (take advice on this) which strengthens the leg muscles. Determination will arise from each player realising the importance of rebounding and making every effort to help his team secure the ball. Technique at the level of starter is fairly straightforward — the defensive player attempts to keep between the offensive player and the basket maintaining an inside position when the shot goes up so that he has the best chance of getting the rebound — a strong wide body position 'blocks out' the attacker's way to basket.

— the offensive player has to work off the ball so that when the shot is attempted he can get into a position to win the rebound. This may mean faking the defender into blocking off the path to basket while he in fact changes to another one and eventually gets the inside position on the defender.

Progression Skills

Alongside possession skills must come progression skills, as we need to get the ball in our possession to the danger area near our opponents' basket. As we have already said the safest and quickest way to achieve this is by good passing — and the coach will always prefer this method of progression. There will be occasions in the game, however, when a pass is not suitable and the player in possession finds himself with the space to move forward.

Alan Baillie takes a good rebound. Notice his team-mate, Vic Tinsley, moving to 'block-out' the opposition number seven

Dribbling

Is used by basketball players to move on the basketball court with the ball in their possession, the move being accompanied by a continuous bouncing of the ball ahead of the player. The two most important uses of the dribble in basketball are:

1. To progress down the court quickly when there is no clear pass readily available.

2. To go round a defender and penetrate toward the basket.

The ability to perform these skills is vital to both starter and top-class player but dribbling is an area of the game where the starter might have great difficulty. Too often the low-level game of basketball is dominated by players dribbling here, there, and everywhere, unaware of passes that could be made, and very often losing possession through loss of control or breaking the rules concerning dribbling.

RULES

There are three key rules the starter should know.
Dribbling means one-handed contact with the ball although the player may alternate hands. Thus he may begin his dribble right-handed but switch to his left to go past a defender. He may not dribbble with two hands together. Once the player has completed a dribble he must pass or shoot — he may not dribble again immediately. Thus defenders work hard to make the dribbler 'pick up' the ball forcing him then to pass the ball to someone else. Defenders also pressure the dribbler in the hope that he will lose control of himself or the ball and cause contact with other players.

Two Hand Rule: 'After giving impetus to the ball the player completes his dribble the instant he touches the ball simultaneously with both hands, or permits the ball to come to rest in one or both hands.'

Double Dribble Rule: 'A player shall not make a second dribble after having completed a dribble, unless the ball...has touched another player.'

Alton Byrd, at one and a half metres (five feet seven inches) dribbles past two metre (six feet seven inches) Danny Randall, by dribbling low and protecting the ball from Randall with his body

Charging Rule: 'A dribbler shall not charge into or contact an opponent in his path...'.

Knowledge of these rules should ensure a controlled and legal dribble, and such dribbles will become successful in a game when the player heeds the three keys to:

SUCCESSFUL DRIBBLING

1. *only* dribble when there is no good pass available.

2. *dribble forward* — a dribble must be a *threat*.

Phil Brazil, Warrington Lada Birchwood Vikings star, dribbles downcourt quickly but under full control as he looks ahead for possible passes. Notice that he is equally skilled with his left hand as he is with his more natural right hand.

3.   Be aware while dribbling forward of other players around — a team-mate might get free under the basket or a second defender might come to mark you.

The dribble must be seen as a link in the total offensive pattern between passing and shooting, and a vital aid to a team being able to keep possession, make progression, and penetrate well enough to create scoring opportunities. If our keys to dribble success are followed the amount of dribbling in the game will be limited, but what there is will be efficient, direct, and a constant threat to the defence.

TECHNIQUE

1.   A dribble goes *forward* so bounce the ball ahead in front of the shoulder of the dribbling hand.

2.   A dribble is *protected* — so dribble with the hand furthest from your defender so your body stays between him and the ball.

3.   A dribble is *controlled* — so bend the knees (not the back) and maintain a low dribble — less chance for errors or stealing. The nearer the defender or the faster the move — the lower the dribble.

4.   A dribble is *not a slap* — so use the fingers to push the ball to the floor, with the wrist and arm being used to control the height and speed of the bounce.

5.   A dribbler is *aware* of what is happening around him — so dribble with your eyes looking ahead of you — not fixed on the ball. Try to develop split vision — seeing the ball and maintaining awareness of what is happening around you.

6.   A dribbler is skilful with *either hand* — so a defender may not over-guard the strong hand and expose the weak one giving him the advantage over the dribbler.

PRACTICE

1.   Continually bouncing a basketball wherever you happen to be — dribbling up and down the stairs at home is an example.

2.   Dribbling in and out of obstacles so that you have to watch where you are going — *head up / awareness* — and use both left and right hands.

3.   Dribbling up and down the court at various speeds and occasionally switching hands.

4.   One versus one dribble against a partner — one dribbles the ball down the court whilst the partner tries to steal it — *no fouls* — and then change over for the return trip.

5.   One versus one drive to basket — practise dribbling around the defender for a lay-up shot. Begin with the defender passive, and then with success change to active defence.

Penetration Skills

When possession and progression have all been achieved there is still one thing left for the player to do — he has to put the ball into the basket. No matter how well a team combines movement, passing and dribbling to get the ball to a scoring position, the final touch must be added for success in basketball — and players and teams will be judged on ability to shoot the ball.

Shooting

Basketball players shoot the ball from two situations. Firstly they shoot when they receive the ball in an open space near enough to the basket for them to believe they will be successful. Very often basketball starters practise and shoot in games from positions outside of their range and not only does the ball miss the basket completely but they ruin the style of the shot in order to make the extra distance — a throw instead of a shot.
    Secondly, players can score when they receive the ball on the move toward basket or have penetrated by dribbling towards the basket. Here starters often suffer from speed without control and rush their shot at basket.

TECHNIQUE
Shooting from a set position and shooting on the move are both difficult skills and require a great deal of practice. It is

extremely important that the correct style of shooting is learned from the very beginning so that every time we practise we are 'grooving' in good and not bad habits. Good shooters are easily recognisable by the fact that they score a high percentage, they shoot in the same manner on each occasion, and they have a certain ease and style in their movements.

There are certain essentials to a good shot at the basket whether stationary or on the move.

1. You must face the basket —
Leave the other stuff to the Globetrotters!

2. You must be balanced and under control —
as a good darts player pauses under perfect control just before he aims and throws, so the basketball player ensures body control and balance at the vital moment that he releases the ball — even if he is on forward movement towards the basket.

3. Eyes on the target —
despite the attentions of the defence concentrate on the target — direct the ball to the line of the target.

4. Total co-ordination —
shooting is a whole body action, starting from the toes and involving whole body extension, and being completed by the most vital part — smooth and full extension of shooting arm, the final snap of the wrist, and a complete follow-through.

5. Shooting arc —
a good shooter arches his shots, never aiming at the ring but always above so that the ball comes down into the hoop — remember

the basketball ring is big enough for two basketballs to be put through at the same time providing they are put through from directly above. A high arc also ensures that a shot that hits the rim might well bounce back up and then back down into the the basket.

6. Confidence —

— a confident shot is the result of many hours of practise and choosing the right time to shoot in the game — these are the qualities of a good shooter who scores most of his shots.

Achieving these is a matter of good technique and a great deal of practice — both in training and playing the game.

Following good possession and progression the aim of penetration is to give an attacker a shot as close to the basket as possible to ensure a high percentage of successes. As defences are too quick to allow an uncontested stationary shot in this area we attempt to score by taking the ball, either from the dribble or from the pass, and shooting while on the move. This shot, where the ball is 'layed-up' against the backboard, is a key weapon in tactical penetration and essential to all starters.

LAY-UP SHOT

With this shot you can score if you get ahead of the defenders (by a quick dribble to basket and lay-up) or by dribbling round a defender to a clear space under the basket — known as driving to the basket.

Although a moving shot, the essence is control before speed and the shot should be made from a strong vertical (high jump) lift following forward momentum, allowing a controlled pause for successful aiming at the target. Important points to consider are:

1. Make sure the area ahead to the basket is clear — don't drive into cover defenders.

2. A firm, quick dribble to basket — but controlled and with head up to maintain awareness.

3. When sufficiently near the basket complete your dribble and take one more firm step.

4. From that base lift upward, stretch body toward rim.

5. Ball firmly held in shooting hand, other hand supporting for control, stretch arm toward rim and push ball softly onto backboard target to deflect into basket. It is best if starters learn to shoot this shot from the right with the right hand, and from the left with the left hand.

6. To make sure that you have achieved a vertical lift (high jump) and shot under control check you have landed virtually under the basket and not beyond the backboard — indicating a long-jump and probably a hurried, off-balance shot.

   A simple method of learning the lay-up shot is known as the *dribble-1-2* technique (see diagram 4).

1. Each starter stands with a ball at a forty-five degrees angle and no more than three steps away from the basket.

2. He then makes three strides into the basket and shoots the lay-up.

N.B. a. when going from right side lead with left foot (which leads to strong, comfortable left foot take-off). Reverse procedure for left side.
      b. good idea to count aloud 'start-1-2' until movement sequence is established.

3. When this is established and good shots are being made consistently, introduce the dribble alongside the first step. The sequence now becomes dribble 1-2 as we make our three steps towards basket. Because

LAY-IN   JUMP   2   1   DRIBBLE

4 The lay-up shot

we are only making one undefended dribble which should be farly low, about fifteen centimetres (six inches), the eyes should never leave the target area — total concentration on good style.

Repeated many times this should become habitual and the starter will have a very valuable attacking weapon at his disposal.

Set Shots

Of course, penetration all the way to the basket is not always possible as the defenders close down the avenues to basket. Then the basketball player has to look for a suitable outside shot, and there are three that may be learned — the two-hand set-shot, the one-handed set-shot and the jump shot. Of these the one-handed set-shot is the most important to the starter as it provides both a good shot and the key to later successful jump shooting. Every successful basketball player at National League level needs a good jump shot but it is a shot that starters find most difficult and they must be patient enough to let it develop naturally from an effective one-hand shot. The two-hand shot is of great use where the shooter is failing from lack of strength. For younger children, girl and women players this is a most useful distance shot and I include it for them. But all starters must progress from two to one-hand set-shot, and from there to jump shots, as soon as they can. Progression, however, cannot be rushed and every good jump shooter has mastered at first a very effective one-hand or two-hand set-shot.

TWO-HAND SET-SHOT

An accurate distance shot that needs time and good body control. In essence this shot is very similar to the chest pass with the exception that from the position of readiness the ball is directed upwards on an arc to basket instead of straight ahead as in a pass.

Main points are:

1.   Balanced set position, facing basket.

2.   Ball firmly controlled in two hands, fingers widespread, thumbs almost meeting behind the ball, elbows into chest.

3.   Eyes on target.

4.   Total body, arm, wrist extension on release.

5.   Follow through.

ONE-HAND SET-SHOT

Though having less range than the two-hand this shot has great accuracy up to six metres (twenty feet) from the basket and, most importantly, can be released slightly quicker giving defenders less chance to rush or block the shot. All starters must work on this shot, beginning close to the basket and, as success and confidence increase, moving further away. Be sure to emphasise smoothness so that the shot is not rushed and the vitally important style and co-ordination are not damaged early in the learning process. Good shooters have ease, consistency, and style — the result of many hours practice and attention to the main points.

1.   Face the basket — eyes, wrist, elbow, knee, leading foot should all be in line with the basket.

2.   Good balanced set position, foot of shooting side slightly ahead of other, knees slightly bent.

POSITION   AIM   UNCOIL   FOLLOW THROUGH
OF   AND
READINESS   SNAP

5 The one hand set-shot

3. Ball transfers from two hands to the main shooting hand behind and slightly under ball, with non-shooting hand supporting balance of ball on the side. Elbow lifts and ball moves up under the chin. The ball is held firmly on the widespread finger tips — not palms of the hands.

4. Total body, arm, and wrist extension on release and follow-through.

5. As part of full extension, weight transfers from back to front foot. The amount of effort from the legs and arm depends on the distance from the basket.

6. Shot is continuous and flowing; co-ordination is very important.

THE JUMP SHOT
   A difficult shot to co-ordinate for the beginner but without doubt the most important shot in the game, because by jumping above defenders a shooter creates his own space and time to make what should be a very controlled shot. It classifies as a set-shot even when taken after movement because of this control from a distance and because the jumper should land back on the spot from which he took off. The starter should not progress

A perfect jump shot as the shooter demonstrates good height in the jump, excellent balance just before release, and a straight line established between basket and ball, wrist, eyes, elbow and body. Notice the defender pressures but does not foul. He scored!

from the one-hand set-shot to a jump shot until he has achieved consistency and success in that and even then should learn and practise the jump shot from close to the basket in the early stages. Technique is very similar to the one-hand set-shot with the exception of the drive from the legs and the release at the top of the jump.

1. Face the basket — eyes, wrist, elbow, knee, shooting foot all lined on basket.

2. Balance — even if after forward dribble body must be balanced prior to release of ball.

3.   Drive upwards with both legs.

4.   Ball, held in shooting hand and supported by non-shooting hand, taken up in front of forehead as elbow lifts prior to extending.

5.   Total body, arm, wrist extension. Follow-through is very important, as much of the body power is taken in the drive upwards.

6.   Release at just about top of jump.

7.   Land back on same spot — not forward on top of defender.

These then are the stationary set-shots that the starter must develop with the recommended progression:

Two-hand set-shot to one-hand set-shot for girls and younger boys. One-hand set-shot to jump shot for older boys and men.

Foul Shots

It is worth noting here the importance of foul shooting. In certain game situations a player will be called upon to shoot 'penalty' shots from the foul shot line. This will happen if the player is fouled when he is in the act of shooting, intentionally fouled by an opponent, fouled after the opposing team has collected eight 'team' fouls, and in certain other special situations. However it happens, it is obviously important that each player is capable of scoring from the foul shot line — many games at National League level are won or lost by foul shooting. It is advisable that the shooter of foul shots shoots his best shot i.e. the ones he practises most (often the one hand set-shot) and does not contrive some special shot for the occasion. It is also advisable that a small part of every practise session is reserved for foul shooting.

Shooting Practise

A good style and constant practise are the keys to successful shooting. A poor style practised often is a bad habit gained so cultivate a good style and practise within your shooting range so that shots are not forced.

1.   One-hand set-shooting under the basket — put your weaker hand behind your back and hold the ball with fingers widespread on stronger hand and under the chin. Bend knees, extend upwards, snap arm and wrist and follow through. Get a high arc on the shot. As you begin to score regularly and easily move out from the basket. Do the same while sitting on a chair.

2.   Continuity shooting — start under the basket, step right and shoot the ball on to the back-board so that it deflects in. Take rebound, step left and do the same that side. Continue and score as many as possible in thirty seconds.

3.   'Round the Clock' shooting — choose seven different line markings around the keyway surrounding the basket and try to go all the way round without missing a shot. Compete with a partner — when you miss he shoots until he misses.

4.   First to five, ten etc. from either side of the court — two teams can compete against each other.

5.   First to twenty-one — a similar game with two points for a basket and one point for scoring your own rebound — there is only one attempt at the rebound.

Chapter Four

Team Tactics

Although the individual skills the starter is learning are vitally important, basketball is essentially a team game and he will have to learn how to co-operate with his team-mates in defending at one end of the court and scoring at the other. To play one's part in a co-ordinated plan of attack or defence, sound fundamental skills are vital but so, too, is the willingness to be part of the team and respond to coaching. The coach has up to ten players to use over the forty minutes of the game with his decision determining which five players will be on court at any one time and how long they will remain there. The beginner may have to wait and work hard at his game before the coach finds the confidence to use him a great deal in the game. It is important to be able to respond to team tactics when out on the court and be part of a team effort designed by the coach in the search for victory.

OFFENSIVE TACTICS

When the coach sends a player on the court he will give him a position to play and certain responsibilities in the team offence. Although I am certain no coach would severely restrict movement — an important principle in successful offence — each coach has to ensure a team balance where each player has space around him to make his moves, i.e. we don't want all five players on one side of the court crowding around the man with the ball. So it is important that the players mostly stay in their allotted positions (see diagram 6). The coach will vary these positions as he attempts to attack different kinds of defences but the principle remains the same — players avoid crowding each other especially near the ball-handler.

Again the offensive responsibilities that a coach may

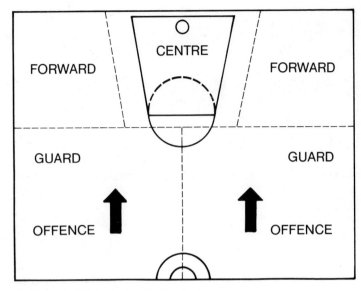

6   Team positions on offence

require of a player will vary according to each situation but there are certain principles of offence that will undoubtedly apply to every situation. I have called these my *five laws of offence* and they apply each time a player receives the ball.

Law 1. The very first thing a player must do when he receives the ball — no matter where he receives it — is to look towards the basket he is attacking to see if there is a team-mate free there to receive a *pass inside* for an early basket. The whole basis of offence is to get the ball to an unmarked player as near to the basket as possible for a high percentage shot (see diagram 7). Obviously teams will not score every time they shoot (a National League team could only expect at most to score five out of ten shots), so it is important that we take our shots from where we are more likely to score i.e. as near the basket as possible. So every time that a player receives the ball he must look towards the basket — often having to turn to face it — and check if anyone is free there for a quick pass. If there is, and the player makes a good quick pass from which his team-mate scores, he is credited with an assist (the pass that leads to the basket) and has played a valuable role in that offence.

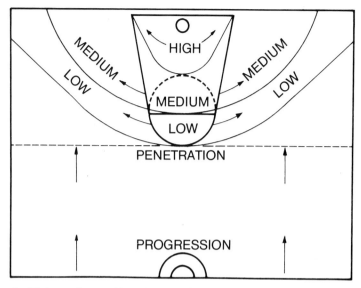

7 High, medium and low shooting percentage areas

Law 2. Obviously follows when, having faced the basket, our attacker with the ball finds there is <u>no one free</u> to receive the ball. However, having looked into the high percentage area he can now ask himself whether he can _penetrate inside,_ past his defender for a driving lay-up. If there is space free under the basket and he can make a quick controlled drive there are good opportunities to score (see diagram 8). With the correct application of the dribble-1-2 drive illustrated in Chapter 3 each player should aim to reach the basket with one dribble from anywhere inside the penetration area (for younger players two quick dribbles). More than one dribble, of course, reduces the speed of the drive and allows other defenders time to move over and either block the pathway to basket or steal the ball.

Law 3. Having checked there is no inside pass available, and then rejected the possibility of a penetration drive, the attacking player must then assess the opportunity to take a _shot at basket_ from the position he is in. It may well be that he can't pass or drive because the defenders have closed in around the basket — therefore his decision could be to shoot. _But_ there is no point in taking a shot that is unlikely to score, so the attacker must be confident

Penetration. The offensive player penetrates through a gap in the defence while the defenders try to close that gap

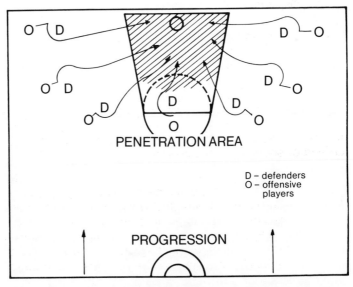

8 Penetration area for driving lay-ups

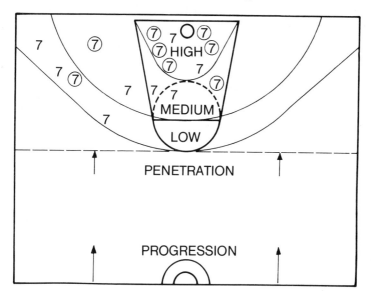

9   Scoring Chart for an individual player —
number seven

Note: the numbers seven indicate where player seven took his shots from
— if circled they show he scored

The statistics reveal player seven scored:

> five out of seven in high percentage area
> two out of five in medium percentage area
> one out of four in low percentage area

Coaching advice to player would be:

> — take shots in high percentage area
> — think carefully in medium percentage area
> —reject shots in low percentage area

he can score from that position. The coach will stress two
criteria of shooting to his players:

    a. , Shooting range — each player must know how
        far from the basket he can shoot comfortably
        and confidently, and stay within it. The coaches
        advice to the player in diagram 9 would be to
        take those shots he gets in the high percentage
        area, think carefully in the medium percentage
        area, but reject all shots in the low percentage
        area.

    b. Shot selection — of the types of shot available,

each player must take those controlled shots within his ability level and reject those hopeful ones which might appear glamorous but only score one out of five or so times.

Law 4. No pass inside, no penetrating drive to the basket, no outside shot, then the attacking player should no longer hold the ball as he is not a threat to the defence but must *pass* immediately to a player in a better position than himself. Ball movement itself is a vital principle of good team offence as good passing will make the defence work, stretch them, and provide the gaps for penetration. While allowing the man with the ball some time to check out his moves, the coach will insist that if none are immediately available the ball must be moved quickly to the next player.

Law 5. Having passed the ball and no longer being a direct threat, the attacker must *reassess his position* on court. The best possible movement would be to cut towards the basket so that he may become the inside target for the man with the ball. If the middle is closed up then he should still make some threatening movement in order to keep his defender's attention — and therefore prevent him 'doubling up' on the man with the ball — and to make himself available again for a pass. All the time the offensive player is without the ball he should be looking for opportunities to make the penetrating cut to the basket and provide the man with the ball an inside pass for an easy basket, as shown in diagram 10.

Once the starter has secured these 'laws' firmly in his mind he will never be lost or indecisive on offence and he will begin to be an effective member of the team. He will still make technical errors but at least they will come from trying to make the right offensive move. The coach of course may predetermine certain patterns and priorities of offence but however complicated they may seem at first they will require the laws outlined above, and if the starter has these fully understood within the coach's total tactics then he is on the way to becoming a valuable team player.

Defensive Tactics

The starter will not be a valuable team member if he can only contribute to scoring baskets and not to preventing the other team scoring. If you score twenty points but the

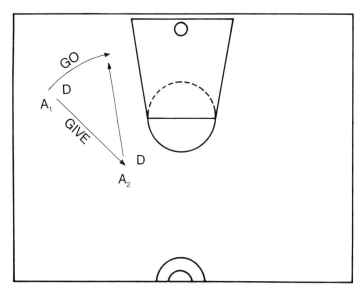

10   Pass and go to basket

Note: Attacker A1 passes ball to A2 and then follows LAW 5 by moving towards the basket, presenting A2 with an easy return pass for a high percentage shot.

man your were marking scores twenty-four points your team is minus four points. So defensive skills are vital to the individual player, and co-ordinated defence is vital to the successful team.

The coach will determine the overall defensive strategy to be used but he will expect each player within the total defensive unit to understand the major principles of defence and be able to carry them out. In a similar way to offence, the success of the team defence is dependent on the skills and abilities of those individuals within the team.

To aid the starter I have established *five laws of defence* which are essential to each individual defender and to all types of team defensive tactics.

Law 1. *Stay between the man you are marking and the basket.* Once the opposition have possession of the ball they will progress it down court and attempt to penetrate by drive or pass as close to the basket as possible for the final shot. The man you are marking will, if he has the ball, attempt to drive past you to the basket or, if he has not got the ball, will attempt to cut to the basket for an inside pass

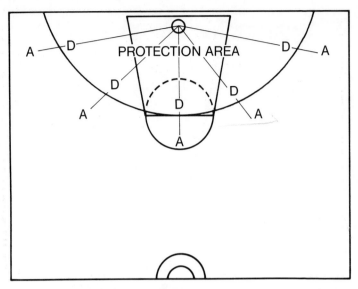

11   Defensive alignment between man and basket

and easy shot. Both are very much more difficult if the defender maintains a position in between his man and the basket at all times, as illustrated in diagram 11.

Law 2. *Defence means the protection of the basket first, your own man or area second.* Law 1 indicates that we must pay particular attention to the man we are marking and ensure we are always in a good position to prevent him threatening the basket. But there are five possible threats to the basket and each defender has to be aware of the other four attackers as well as his own man. So, in addition to taking up a position where he is in between his man and the basket, the defender must also adopt a position where he can see what is happening around him. Diagram 12 illustrates this clearly. When A2 has the ball all of D2's attention is on marking him but defenders D1 and D3 have the split responsibility of marking their man and protecting the basket high-percentage area from people cutting or driving into it; their position must be such that they can see both their man and the ball.

If all the individual defenders have this law firmly in mind it will mean that the attacker with the ball will always have to face 'cover' defence if he does beat his man, and that attacking players cutting into the high-percentage

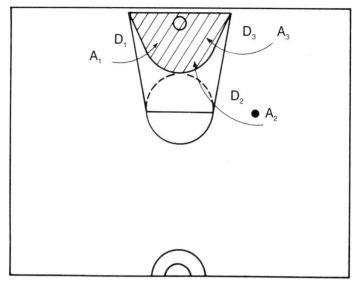

12 Protecting the basket

area near the basket will find other defenders there denying the space. Diagram 13 shows how a good defence responds to the threat to the basket of A1 when he has the ball. Obviously he is marked tightly as is A3 and A2 — the nearest men for a threatening pass — but A4 and A5 are not threatening the basket so their defenders have moved over to help stop the threat to the basket from the ball side of the court. If the ball were passed round to A5 the whole defence would move out to counteract the new threat. Each player thus defends basket first, man or area second.

Law 3. *Get back to basket first.* Laws 1 and 2 emphasise very clearly the need for correct positioning for the defence to succeed. For correct positioning to be established defenders need to get back to the basket they are protecting before the attackers have progressed the ball into the penetration area. All good offences will be looking to move the ball quickly down court and get ahead of the defence for an easy 'cheap' basket, and the defence must prevent this by getting into position before an attack can be mounted. Defence begins the moment your team loses possession and it must become a habit of all players

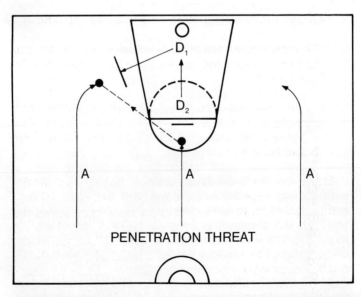

13 Cover defence

14 Tandem defence

to get back quickly in defence. Players on the fringe of the offence — usually the guards — will find this easier than the others and they should drop back quickly and adopt the position shown in diagram 14 where they are protecting the basket and delaying their opponents' fast break. If D1 moves out to stop the threat from the side, D2 will drop to the basket — the basket must always be protected and the first man back must always go straight to the basket. When the other defenders have arrived D1 and D2 will switch to their particular defensive responsibilities.

Law 4. *Defence means pressure.* Defence means pressurizing the opponents into giving up the ball, committing a violation, or taking a poor shot at basket. As the attacking team only have thirty seconds of possession before they must take a shot it means a short period of sustained pressure from the defending team. The coach might ask the team to apply that pressure all over the court — full court pressing defence — or he may only require it nearer the basket they are protecting — half court pressing defence. It is important the starter knows where and when to apply that pressure.

Three simple rules may help here:

1. Always pressure your man when he has the ball.

2. The closer your man is to the basket, the closer you are to him — the further he is the further you may be from him.

3. If your man cuts into the high-percentage area then you must increase defensive pressure on him in order to prevent him receiving an inside pass for a close shot at basket.

Starters often make the mistake of confusing pressure with fouling — wasted fouls will hurt the team both in losing individual players with five fouls and in collecting eight team fouls quickly. Defenders should note that it is the exception to actually steal the ball off an opponent, and far more the rule to pressurise him into error that will eventually give you possession back.

Law 5. *Every defender must be a rebounder.* If our defenders get back on defence quickly, take and maintain

Jimmy Macauley (nine) with nowhere to go as Crystal Palace exert good defensive pressure with four of their players surrounding the ball. Alton Byrd (thirteen) shows clearly how to exert maximum pressure without fouling

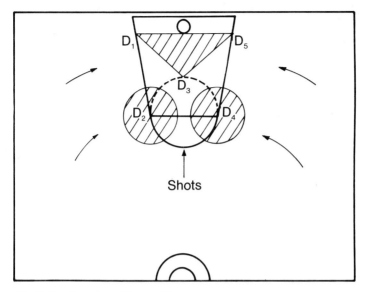

Shots

15 Defensive rebounding position

good position, and exert great pressure on the offence, there will be many occasions when the offence will take a hurried shot and fail to score. In order to benefit from all this work it is essential we convert that missed shot into our possession by securing the defensive rebound. This should not be too difficult a task for the defender for if he has maintained good position he will already be in between his man and the basket. His task is then to 'box out' his opponent so that he maintains the best position for the rebound. Diagram 15 illustrates normal defensive rebounding positions with especial emphasis on the job of the defenders close to the basket — the expected area of rebound — to close together and secure a solid rebound triangle. The outer defenders must prevent their men from taking the occasional high rebound which bounces quite a long way out from the basket.

These five laws are essential to good individual and team defence. Basically the coach will organise his team into either a man for man defence — where each player marks one of the opposition — or a zone defence — where each player defends within a certain area surrounding the basket. Now the laws are the essential basis of man for man defence and are generally understood within this

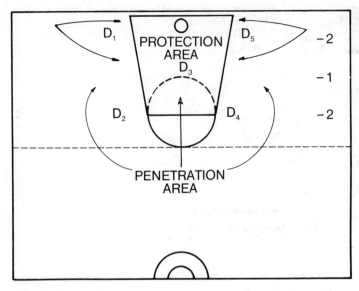

16   2-1-2 zone defence

context, but they also apply very firmly to zone defence and this is less well understood. If we take as an example a 2-1-2 zone defence and then see how the laws apply we should see their relevance more clearly. Diagram 16 illustrates the basic line-up of a 2-1-2 defence and their defensive areas. If we get law 3 out of the way first, obviously to get into these positions before the offence launches its attack, the defence *must get back quickly.*

Now law 1 indicates that defenders must be in between the attackers and the basket and law 2 adds that the defender must always first protect the basket from any threat offered. If the team stays as illustrated in diagram 16 then these two laws may be broken — so the zone defence must move and be fluid in order to satisfy laws 1 and 2. Diagram 17 shows this zone movement in action when A1 has the ball. There is a defender between each man and the basket (law 1) and notice how D4 and D5 have moved in from their areas in order to first and foremost protect the basket from any threat from A1 — with the ball — or A3 and A2 — the two men most likely to receive a pass from A1 and become a threat (law 2).

The only law left unsatisfied so far is law 4 — the law of

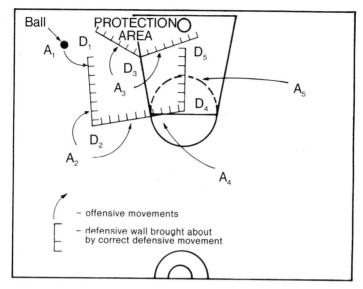

17   Defensive movement

pressure — but the movement of the zone has brought great pressure to bear on the offence. The ball handler A1 is marked very tightly — as are A2 and A3, the closest men to the ball, while the off the ball basket protection of D4 and D5 means that the high percentage area is very well protected and the offence is outnumbered five to three on the ball side of the court — pressure indeed! As the ball moves, of course, the defence adjusts and our laws are constantly being satisfied to give the offence the least possible chance to secure an easy basket.

Thus, regardless of the defensive organisation imposed by the coach, if the starter understands and follows the laws on defence he should prove to be a valuable individual and team defender.

By now our starters should have acquired a thorough understanding of the principles and practice of basketball. This book has treated the game in a very simple manner and I advise the player, teacher or coach to do likewise; success in basketball comes from doing simple things well! Nevertheless, success will not come without hard work and I hope that this book has given the beginner plenty to concentrate on. For the starter who learns quickly more advanced instruction will be covered in a further book.

Finally, I hope that basketball gives you as much pleasure as it has given me. Good Luck!